Materials

Metal

Chris Oxlade

www.heinemann.co.uk/library
Visit our website to find out more information about **Heinemann Library** books.

To Order:
 Phone 44 (0) 1865 888066
 Send a fax to 44 (0) 1865 314091
 Visit the Heinemann Library Bookshop at www.heinemann.co.uk/library to browse our catalogue and order online.

First published in Great Britain by Heinemann Library, Halley Court, Jordan Hill, Oxford OX2 8EJ
a division of Reed Educational and Professional Publishing Ltd.
Heinemann is a registered trademark of Reed Educational & Professional Publishing Ltd.

OXFORD MELBOURNE AUCKLAND JOHANNESBURG BLANTYRE
GABORONE IBADAN PORTSMOUTH (NH) USA CHICAGO

© Reed Educational and Professional Publishing Ltd 2002
The moral right of the proprietor has been asserted.

Designed by Storeybooks
Originated by Ambassador Litho Ltd.
Printed and bound in Hong kong/China

ISBN 0 431 12722 0 (hardback)   ISBN 0 431 12729 8 (paperback)
05 04 03 02   06 05 04 03 02
10 9 8 7 6 5 4 3 2   10 9 8 7 6 5 4 3 2 1

British Library Cataloguing in Publication Data
  Oxlade, Chris
  Metal. – (Materials)
  1. Metal
  I. Title
  620.1'6

Acknowledgements
Corbis /Peter Johnson p.16, /Paul A.Souders p.14, /Yogi Inc. p.15; D.I.Y. Photo Library p.23, /Photodisc p.24; Edifice p.7; Photodisc pp.6, 17, 19; PPL Library p.11; Rolls Royce PLC p.25; Still Pictures /David Drain p.27, /Mark Edwards pp 12, 13, 26, /Thomas Raupach pp,4, 29; Stone p.18; Tudor Photography pp.5, 22; Zul Mukhida p.8.

Cover photograph reproduced with permission of Tudor Photography.

Every effort has been made to contact copyright holders of any material reproduced in this book. Any omissions will be rectified in subsequent printings if notice is given to the Publisher.

Contents

You can find words shown in bold, **like this**, in the Glossary.

What is metal?

A metal is a hard, shiny material. There are dozens of different metals. Metals are found in rocks in the ground. This metal is aluminium. It has just been made into thin sheets.

People make many useful things from metals. They are called metal objects. Everything you can see here is made from metal.

Hard and soft

Some metals are very hard and very strong. It is difficult to cut and bend them. The cutting edge, or blade, of this **saw** is made of a very hard metal called **steel**.

Some metals, such as lead, are softer and quite weak. It is easy to cut or bend them. In some countries, builders use strips of lead on roofs. The lead keeps water out.

Electricity and heat

Most metals let **electricity** flow
through them easily. They are good
conductors of electricity. The **lightbulb**
will glow when electricity flows through
the aluminium foil.

Metals are also good at letting heat flow through them. They are called good conductors of heat. Metal cooking pans let heat flow from the cooking ring to the food inside.

Metals and magnets

Some metal things stick to **magnets**. In this fishing game, you use a magnet on the end of a string to pick up fish shapes. This is because the fish are made from paper and have a metal paper clip.

The only everyday metals that stick to magnets are **iron** and **steel**. The paper clips in the fishing game are made of steel. So are lots of cans. Most metals do not stick to magnets.

Where metals come from

Metals are found in some rocks in the ground. The rocks are called **ores**. Miners break up the rocks with tools and **explosives**. Huge diggers load the broken rocks into trucks.

The rock is worked on to get the metal out. This is called processing. To get **iron** from iron ore, the ore is **melted** in a hot **furnace**. The runny iron flows out of the bottom of the furnace.

Shaping metals

Metals can be bent and hammered to make different shapes. This blacksmith heats **iron** until it glows red to make it soft. Then he shapes it by hitting it with a hammer.

Metals can also be cut into shapes with tools such as **drills** and **saws**. The parts of the tools that do the cutting are made from very hard metals.

Rusting

If **iron** or **steel** things are left out in the wet, they go brown and flaky. The iron slowly turns into a new material called **rust**. Metals such as gold and silver stay shiny because they do not rust.

Rust damages iron and steel things. It makes them crumble. You can stop things going rusty by painting them, or by coating them with another metal called zinc. This stops water getting through.

Metals for electricity

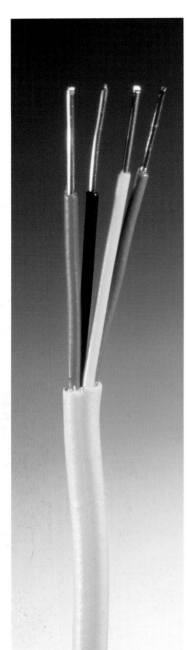

Cables like these that carry **electricity** around a house have wires in them. The wires are made of copper. The cables are covered in plastic to stop the electricity getting from one wire to another.

Inside machines such as computers, electricity travels along thin copper tracks on a plastic board. A metal called **solder** can be used to fix the parts, or components, to the board.

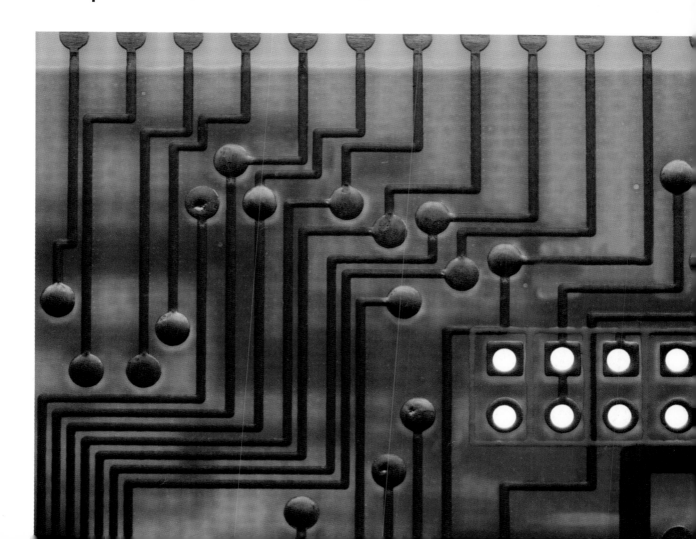

Iron and steel

Iron is the most common metal we use. It is shaped by **melting** it and pouring it into moulds. This is called casting, and the iron is called cast iron. Here you can see a cast iron drain cover.

Steel is made from iron mixed with tiny amounts of other materials. It is much stronger than iron. Many things, such as tools, cars and the frames that hold some buildings up, are made from steel.

Aluminium and copper

The thin foil used to wrap food in the kitchen is made of a metal called aluminium. Aluminium is lighter than **iron** or **steel**. It is also used to make cooking pans and some cans.

Copper is a reddish-brown metal used to make the wire in **electricity** cables. Water pipes are made from copper, too, because it does not go rusty like iron or steel.

Alloys

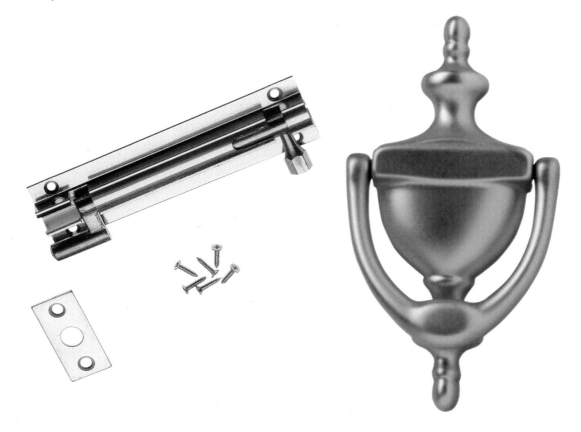

An **alloy** is a metal made by mixing two or more metals together. Alloys are harder and stronger than the metals they are made from. Brass is an alloy of copper and zinc.

Aeroplane builders use alloys that are very strong but very light in weight. Aeroplane bodies and engines are made from alloys that contain metals called aluminium, nickel and titanium.

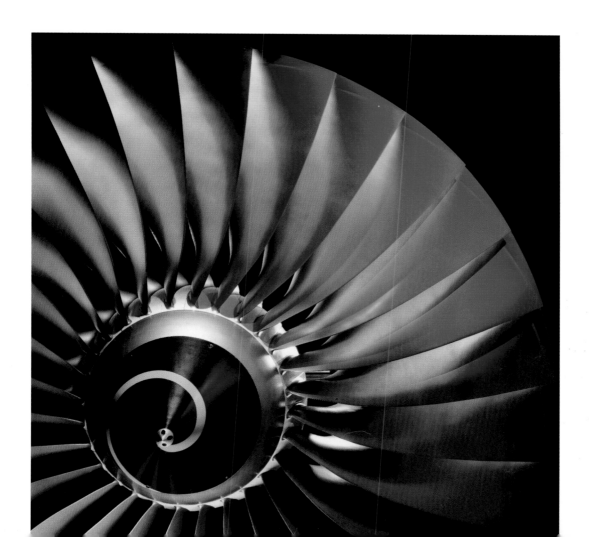

Recycling metals

A lot of the rubbish we throw away is made of metal. It takes a lot of **energy** to make metals. This energy is wasted if the metals are thrown away.

Most metals can be used again, or recycled, instead of being thrown away. If people throw old metal things into special bins, the metal can be collected. Then it is **melted** down and made into new things.

Fact file

▶ Metals are hard, shiny materials.

▶ Metals feel smooth and cold.

▶ Some metals are very hard and very strong. Some metals are softer and weaker.

▶ All metals allow **electricity** to flow through them.

▶ All metals allow heat to flow through them.

▶ **Iron** and **steel** are metals that stick to **magnets**. Most metals do not stick to magnets.

▶ Most metals do not float.

Would you believe it?

Lumps of gold are sometimes found in rock. These lumps are called nuggets. The largest gold nugget ever found weighed an amazing 70 kilograms. That's as heavy as an adult person!

Glossary

alloy   metal made by mixing two metals

conductor   material that lets electricity or heat flow through it

drill   tool for making holes in pieces of material

electricity   form of energy. We use electricity to make electric machines work.

energy   energy is needed to make things happen. For example, you need energy to move about.

explosive   something that explodes, or blows up, when it is heated

factory   place where things are made using machines

furnace   container, like a huge oven, inside which materials are melted

iron shiny, grey metal used to make millions of different objects

magnet object that attracts iron or steel

melt heat a material until it turns from solid to liquid

ore rock that metals are found in. It is dug from the ground.

rust brown, flaky material that appears on iron or steel when it is left in the wet. We then say that the iron or steel is rusty.

saw tool for cutting bits of material into pieces. It has a sharp, jagged cuting edge.

solder alloy, often made of copper and zinc. It is used to join electrical parts.

steel metal made mostly from iron. Steel is stronger than iron.

More books to read

Images: Materials and their Properties
Big Book Compilation
Heinemann Library, 1999

Science All Around Me: Materials
Karen Bryant-Mole
Heinemann Library, 1996

Science Explorers: Metal
A & C Black, 1999

Find Out About. . . Metal
Henry Pluckrose
Franklin Watts UK

Index